Shadow and Light
TADAO ANDO AT THE CLARK

Shadow and Light
TADAO ANDO AT THE CLARK

Essay by Michael Webb
Principal Photography by Richard Pare

Clark Art Institute
Williamstown, Massachusetts

Distributed by Yale Universty Press
New Haven and London

Published on the occasion of the opening of the Clark Center, July 4, 2014

Produced by the Publications Department of the Clark Art Institute, 225 South Street, Williamstown, Massachusetts 01267
clarkart.edu

Thomas J. Loughman, *Associate Director of Program and Planning*
Anne Roecklein, *Managing Editor*
Dan Cohen, *Special Projects Editor*
Hannah Rose Van Wely, *Publications Assistant*
Walker Downey, *Publications Intern*

Copyedited and proofread by Lucy Gardner Carson
Designed by David Edge
Printed by SPC Marcom Studio,
North Springfield, Vermont

Distributed by Yale University Press, 302 Temple Street, P.O. Box 209040, New Haven, Connecticut 06520-9040
yalebooks.com/art

Printed and bound in the United States of America
10 9 8 7 6 5 4 3 2 1

Library of Congress Cataloging-in-Publication Data
Sterling and Francine Clark Art Institute.
  Shadow and light: Tadao Ando at the Clark / essay by Michael Webb ; principal photography by Richard Pare.
    pages cm
  "Published on the occasion of the opening of the Clark Center, July 4, 2014."
  ISBN 978-1-935998-18-1 (sterling and francine clark art institute, publisher : alk. paper)—ISBN 978-0-300-20788-0 (yale university press, distributor : alk. paper)
  1. Ando, Tadao, 1941– Criticism and interpretation.
  2. Sterling and Francine Clark Art Institute—Buildings.
  3. Art museum architecture—Massachusetts—Williams-town. 4. Williamstown (Mass.)—Buildings, structures, etc. I. Pare, Richard. II. Webb, Michael, 1937– Reimag-ined Clark. III. Title.
  N867.A88 2014
  727'.7097441—dc23
                              2014016485

All photographs by Richard Pare except the following: Mike Agee: pp. 34–36; Tucker Bair: p. 11 (top left and bottom right); Jonas Dovydenas: p. 18 (bottom); © Jeff Goldberg / Esto: pp. 31, 32–33 (left); Kenneth Kennefick: p. 33 (far right); Kris Qua: pp. 2, 12–13, 17 (bottom left), 18 (top), 27 (top right), 41, 49 (far right), 50–57, 58–59 (left), 60 (top left), 61, 62 (far left); Victoria Saltzman: pp. 17 (top left), 60 (bottom left)

Additional Credits:
El Anatsui, *Intermittent Signals,* 2009, The Broad Art Foundation, © El Anatsui: p. 36; © Estate of Juan Muñoz: pp. 34–35; Courtesy of Tadao Ando and Associates: pp. 28–29, 38–39

DIRECTOR'S FOREWORD

In 2001, the Clark Art Institute's trustees approved a master plan developed by Cooper, Robertson, and Partners to address the Clark's future programmatic and infrastructure needs. In the same year, Pritzker Prize–winning architect Tadao Ando was selected to realize the first phase of that plan, and he presented his design to the community in 2003. After extensive discussion and refinement, the Institute's first Ando building, recently named the Lunder Center at Stone Hill, was completed in 2008. It provides intimate exhibition galleries along with a conference and studio art facility for the Clark, as well as a state-of-the-art home for the Williamstown Art Conservation Center. A broad terrace with an outdoor café overlooking the Green Mountains of Vermont offers visitors to Williamstown an architectural site with a spectacular vista.

The Clark Center, completed in 2014, is the heart of Ando's vision for the Institute. Beautifully integrated with the surrounding landscape, the building enhances both the visitor's experience of the Clark's 140-acre campus and the Institute's ability to fulfill its dual mission as both an art museum and a center for research and higher education. By providing 11,000 square feet of new gallery space for special exhibitions, a multipurpose pavilion for conferences, lectures, and events, as well as new dining, retail, and family orientation spaces, the Clark Center ensures that the Institute will remain a place to experience great works of art and a site for scholarship and critical debate.

I am extremely grateful to Mr. Ando and to Gensler, the project's executive architects, as well as the many talented and hardworking staff and consultants who have participated in realizing this extraordinary enhancement of the Clark Art Institute.

ARCHITECT'S STATEMENT

TADAO ANDO

Thirteen years have passed since I first visited the Clark Art Institute in 2001 and began work on the Clark's campus expansion project. Thanks to the support and encouragement from director Michael Conforti, diligent staff members of the Institute, the community of Williamstown, and the collaboration of local design team members and contractors, this project has remained in my heart all the time, and has proceeded without any compromises throughout such a long period.

The architecture aims to embody the Clark's unique concept of engagement with art in a rich natural environment. The buildings were designed to become a part of the landscape and to make visitors conscious of nature's seasonal changes. I wish to create a space that will motivate visitors and artists to be free-minded and creative.

Stone Hill Center was opened in 2008, and this summer, the Clark Center will complete the campus expansion project and signal a new start for the Clark. My hope is that this new building, standing on an undulating 140-acre campus, will encourage flexible and diverse encounters between art, nature, and people.

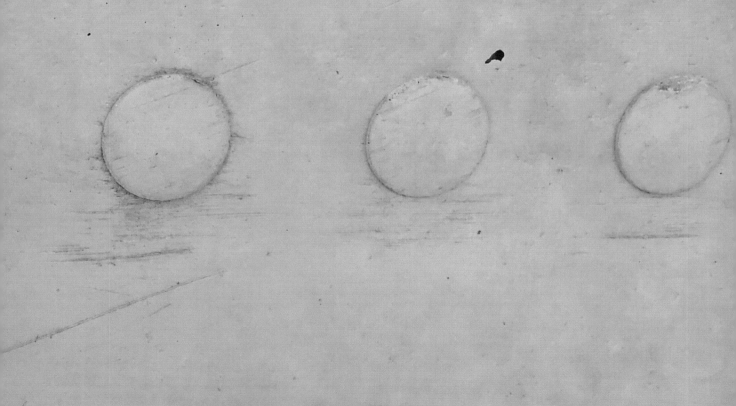

THE REIMAGINED CLARK:
TRANSFORMING THE EXPERIENCE OF
ARCHITECTURE, ART, AND NATURE

MICHAEL WEBB

THE CLARK ART INSTITUTE is one of the most respected art institutions in the world. Widely known for its intimate galleries and stunning natural environment, the Clark defines itself by its dual mission as both a public art museum and a center for higher education. The interrelated aspects of the Institute's character are exemplified by the quality of its art, the depth of its commitment to the generation of ideas, and the beauty of its pastoral setting.

When the Clark opened in 1955, it consisted of the white marble Museum Building designed by Daniel Perry. In 1973, Pietro Belluschi's red granite building (named the Manton Research Center in 2007) was added. A master plan for the 140-acre campus was commissioned from Cooper, Robertson, and Partners in the late 1990s; this was approved in 2001. In that same year, the Japanese architect Tadao Ando was invited to plan and design two complementary buildings: Stone Hill Center—recently named the Lunder Center at Stone Hill—which made its debut in 2008, and the newly completed Clark Center. These additions, combined with a thoughtful remodeling of the existing buildings and a long-term enhancement of the landscape, enrich the Clark experience for lovers of art and nature, curators, scholars from near and far, students, and local residents alike.

In 2000, Clark director Michael Conforti toured the world in search of architects with the skill and sensitivity to create buildings that would open up possibilities for future generations. A committee selected Tadao Ando, who was chosen for the rigor and reticence of his work, his feeling for light and landscape, and a gift for simplicity that echoes the Shaker legacy and the frugal New England vernacular. His first important works in the United States were the Pulitzer Foundation for the Arts in Saint Louis and the Modern Art Museum of Fort Worth. These projects demonstrated that the finely crafted concrete of his Japanese buildings could be matched by American builders, and they showed how successfully he could work on different scales. Ando's buildings have a strong sense of place, but he employs a similar vocabulary at home and abroad. Traditional Japanese ideas—of unfolding vistas, first concealed and then revealed through a framed opening, of shifting axes, and a oneness with the earth—merge seamlessly with the geometry of Western modernism.

Born in Osaka in 1941, Ando began his adult life as a professional boxer. He developed an early love of carpentry and taught himself about architecture as he traveled the world, finding inspiration in the work of Frank Lloyd Wright, Le Corbusier, Alvar Aalto, and Louis Kahn. "It is more important that I learn things through my own body and spirit than through books," says Ando. "By going abroad I became closer to both Japan and foreign countries, and the things inside me and the things outside me intermingle and stimulate each other."

"I want to create intense yet quiet buildings where the voice of their creator can be heard," Ando adds, "and to realize spaces . . . that promote conversations with natural materials, where one can feel light, air, and rain." Over the past six years, the Lunder Center at Stone Hill has fulfilled all of these goals. It was conceived as a sanctuary in the woods, to be discovered at the end of a winding path; a contemplative retreat with two small galleries and a terrace café that invites visitors to gaze out to the Green Mountains and the Taconic Range. Visitors can also watch conservators at work in the Williamstown Art Conservation Center, the largest regional conservation center in the country, which restores paintings and objects from fifty-five other institutions in the Northeast. The Lunder Center's steel and concrete block is partially clad with red cedar boards that are weathering to a soft gray, complementing the concrete that was poured into forms lined with pine boards etched with acid to accentuate the pattern of the grain.

For the Clark Center, Ando initially wanted to use smooth concrete as a foil to the white marble of the museum and the dark red granite of the Manton building. Instead, he was persuaded to employ granite from the same quarry that had supplied the Manton Research Center forty years earlier. Textured and richly grained, the granite covers three walls that enclose and bisect the interiors and terraces to the south. Sunlight brings out the random patterns of the stone panels, and in wet weather the exterior surfaces darken to the tone of porphyry, echoing the purplish hues of the surrounding hills. A sharp angle frames a green roof that doubles as a sculpture terrace.

"The Clark Center is the keystone of the whole project," says Tom Loughman, associate director of program and planning. "It reorients one's experience of the campus, shifting the emphasis to the landscape. It provides purpose-designed visitor amenities to replace ad hoc facilities in the older buildings. We always had a public mission—now we can express it clearly. And the building offers flexible, modular spaces for a variety of high-caliber exhibitions."

Ando's initial design for the Clark Center called for a two-story building, a separate restaurant and conference center, and parking for 400 cars beneath a shallow pool. His proposal proved more ambitious and costly than the Clark desired, so the architectural team relocated parking to a landscaped lot and distilled the public amenities into a pair of single-story pavilions, concealed behind a boundary wall, which open onto waterfront terraces. The west pavilion doubles as a gallery and conference space that is adaptable to special events. A glazed entry vestibule links this to the reception area and museum shop, with a free-floating staircase descending to a wedge of lofty galleries and a café, both naturally lit from sunken courtyards. This is a feature Ando has used previously to great effect; for example, in the subterranean Benetton house in Treviso, Italy, and the Chichu Museum on the island of Naoshima in the Inland Sea of Japan. Ando's close collaborator, Kulapat Yantrasast, who now heads the architectural firm wHY, designed the store and café furnishings, which were crafted from local New England woods.

The promenade that leads from the parking lot to the main entrance, down to the galleries, and out to the terraces culminates in a gentle ramp that ascends to a glass-walled lobby and a new entry in the rear wall of the Museum Building. This puts visitors on the same east-west axis as the original entry through the front portico, which was closed when the red granite building was added.

For years the entry was skewed to a bridge on the south side, betraying the logic of the Beaux-Arts plan.

Selldorf Architects of New York, which has been acclaimed for its transformation of a Manhattan townhouse into the Neue Galerie and recently won a commission to design a ground-up art museum in San Diego, was invited to refurbish and remodel galleries in both of the Clark's old buildings. "The design changes may appear subtle to some, but they required precision and restraint at all times," explains firm principal Annabelle Selldorf. "The result will better serve the Clark's dual mission and enhance the visitor's experience of the permanent collection."

To improve the flow of visitor circulation, openings replaced period room–style fireplaces in the galleries overlooking Schow Pond, and the corridor that separated these galleries from the central galleries was divided up to transform this linear space into a sequence of intimate rooms. The rectangular former entry lobby was turned into a square sculpture court, allowing the flanking spaces to grow in size and become elegant galleries for porcelain and other decorative arts, displayed in cabinets that were also designed by Selldorf. Offices were reconfigured into gallery spaces, so that the entire main floor of the Museum Building is now dedicated to art. Glass in the drop ceilings that diffuses light from roof lanterns was cleaned or replaced, mechanical services were updated, and discreet LED track lighting was substituted for spotlights (one curator likened the old spots to automobile headlights). Selldorf worked closely with the Clark throughout the process—discussions on the colors to be used on the walls continued until a month or two before the opening—and demonstrated a sincere appreciation of just how much has been invested in this extraordinary collection since it was transferred from the founders' apartment and storage spaces, nearly sixty years ago.

In the Manton Research Center, Selldorf converted the atrium into a reading room that serves the 350,000-volume art library and is accessible to all. Leading out of this soaring space is the new Manton Study Center for Works on Paper, a bookstore, and a coffee bar. "The two buildings are very different and idiosyncratic," Selldorf observes. "It was important that each should maintain its separate character, while becoming a more coherent unit."

For the curators, the new and improved galleries open up an exciting array of possibilities for rethinking the permanent collection and mounting a much wider range of temporary exhibitions. "We will now be able to display sixty percent of our collection, and ninety-five percent of what most

people want to see," says Richard Rand, the Robert and Martha Lipp Senior Curator. The Clark's thirty-two Renoirs will remain in the central gallery, sharing the space with Rodin sculptures. Paintings by Winslow Homer and Frederic Remington will be moved to the opening room, and the treasured Piero della Francesca will be given a position with better light. The Ando galleries have seventeen-foot-high ceilings and sharp angles that will challenge and inspire Rand and his colleagues to make best use of them.

Most of the artworks in the Clark's collection, which range from the Italian Renaissance to French Impressionism by way of nineteenth-century American masters, were solitary acts of creation. Ando approaches each of his architecture projects like an artist, sketching a plan or elevation with the confidence of an Abstract Expressionist or a calligrapher brushing ink onto paper. But everything that follows is a team effort, for architecture is a collaborative art, and construction is exponentially more so. As executive architects, the New York office of Gensler drew on their own experience and design skills to oversee the work of Ando, Selldorf, and landscape architecture firm Reed Hilderbrand, two contractors, and a score of consultants. Establishing a productive relationship with Ando, who speaks no English, was a challenge at first for Gensler partner Madeline Burke-Vigeland and senior associate David Adler. They began by exchanging drawings. Burke-Vigeland likens the process to a chess match, with a constant alternation of moves, as Gensler turned Ando's sketches into working drawings, staying true to his intentions while also meeting the needs of the Clark. They established a relationship of trust, allowing both sides to win.

Landscape architect Gary Hilderbrand of Boston-based Reed Hilderbrand came on board in September 2001, soon after Ando was appointed. His deep personal experience of the New England landscape helped him to conserve and enhance the Clark campus, which he describes as a complicated landscape, from the front lawn to pasture and woods, with wetlands, varied patterns of drainage, difficult soils, and neighboring properties to consider. He sketched a network of footpaths, "less to connect buildings than to open up the entire campus and weave the parts together," he says, adding, "We picked up everything and put it back, carefully, in slightly different places."

Central to Ando's design was the idea of replacing the former parking lot with a shallow reflecting pool, divided in three by weirs and flanked by weeping willows. "The challenge was to make it a pleasing shape that fit with the land and became a key part of our water-use plan," Hilderbrand says.

The pool is complete; the newly planted grasses, maples, oaks, tulip poplars, and sweet gums will take many more years to mature.

Sustainability was a high priority, and it's achieved unobtrusively—there are no arrays of photo-voltaic panels. Much of the power is generated from geothermal wells, and the ground-hugging Clark Center absorbs heat through its thermal mass. Rainwater and snowmelt are collected at different points on the campus, stored and filtered, cutting the Clark's consumption of potable mains water by half. The pool can be replenished from a reservoir that stores surplus groundwater, and any discharge is biologically cleansed in the lower basin and adjacent wetlands. As a result of these and other provisions, the Clark expects to secure a LEED Silver certification for its new center.

"We were not just adding a building, but rather creating a new experience for visitors that enhances the programmatic impact of the Clark," explains Michael Conforti. Visitors drive in, follow a picturesque meandering path, and then enjoy a moment of revelation, all the more impressive for its having been delayed. The Clark has become a model of its kind, with exemplary architecture enhancing the viewing and study of art.

LUNDER CENTER AT STONE HILL

OPENED IN 2008, THE LUNDER CENTER AT STONE HILL houses exhibition galleries, a conference room, and the Williamstown Art Conservation Center—the largest regional conservation center in the country. Located on a wooded hillside, it includes a seasonal café and a terrace that has magnificent views of the Taconic Range and Green Mountains.

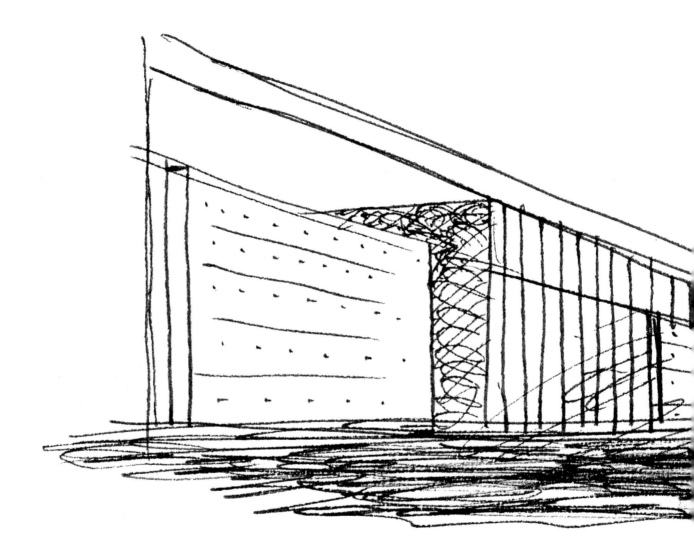

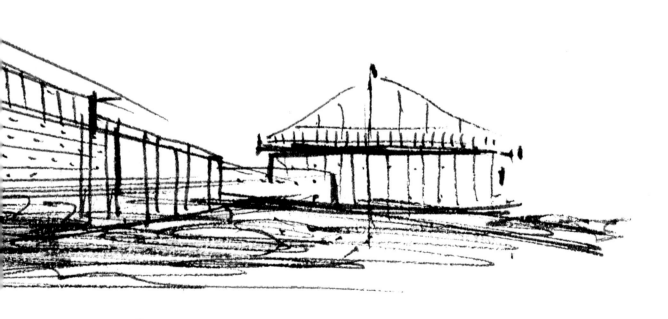

SITUATED AT THE HEART OF THE CAMPUS, THE CLARK CENTER provides the Institute with 11,000 square feet of new exhibition galleries, a multipurpose pavilion, public education spaces, and expanded café and museum shop facilities. Seamlessly integrated into the Clark's existing architecture and bordered on the south end by reflecting pools, the Clark Center innovatively enhances the visitor's campus experience both inside and outside the building.

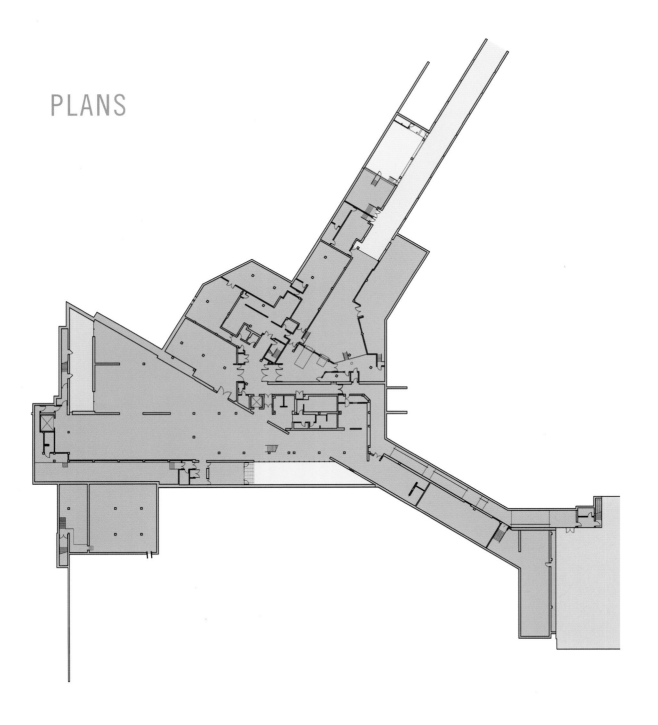

PLANS

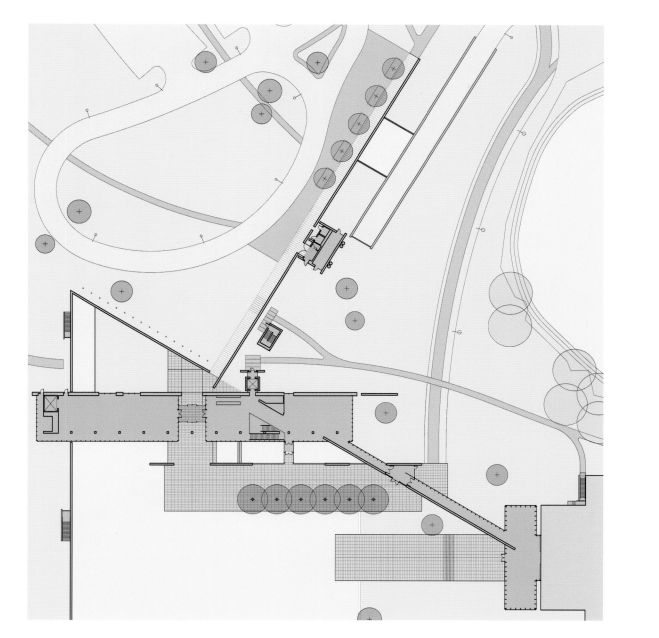

INPUTS

 1 SURFACE DRAINS

2 FOUNDATION DRAIN

3 GEOTHERMAL WELLS

4 POTABLE WATER

5 RAINWATER

OUTPUTS

1 IRRIGATION

2 PLUMBING

3 HEATING + COOLING

4 WATER FEATURE

5 OVERFLOW TO INFILTRATION

6 EMERGENCY OVERFLOW TO X-MAS BROOK

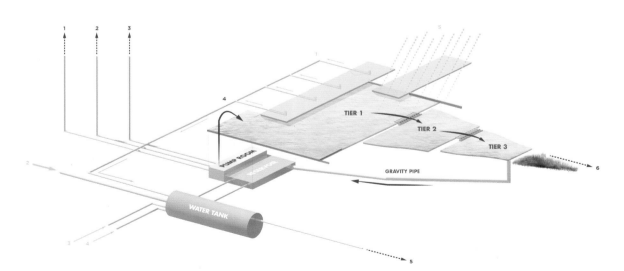

TIER 1

TIER 2

TIER 3

PUMP ROOM

WATER TANK

GRAVITY PIPE

LUNDER CENTER
AT STONE HILL

STONE HILL
MEADOW

FOREST

TERRACED
POOLS

CLARK
CENTER

MANTON
RESEARCH
CENTER

MUSEUM
BUILDING

SCHOW
POND

SOUTH STREET

PROJECT TEAM

Design Architect
Tadao Ando and Associates
Osaka, Japan

Landscape Architect
Reed Hilderbrand Associates
Watertown, Massachusetts

Architect of Record
Gensler
New York, New York

Consulting Architect
wHY Architects
Los Angeles, California

Terraced Pool Designer
Dan Euser Waterarchitecture
Richmond Hill, Ontario

Construction Manager
Turner Construction Company
Albany, New York

Civil Engineer
Guntlow & Associates
Williamstown, Massachusetts

Structural Engineer
Buro Happold
New York, New York

MEP / Fire Protection Engineer
AltieriSeborWieber
Norwalk, Connecticut

Lighting / Acoustics Consultant
Arup
New York, New York

Enclosure Consultant
James R. Gainfort Consulting
Architects
New York, New York

Concrete Consultant
Reginald D. Hough, FAIA
Rhinebeck, New York

Code Consultant
Technical Solution Associates
Jefferson, Massachusetts

AV Consultant
Shen Milson & Wilke
New York, New York

Food Facilities Consultants
Manask & Associates
Burbank, California
Clevenger Frable LaVallee
White Plains, New York

Program Consultant
Lord Cultural Resources
Toronto, Ontario

Cost Estimator
Stuart-Lynn Company
New York, New York

Owner Representatives
Arcadis U.S.
Chicago, Illinois
Zubatkin Owner Representation
New York, New York

Project Management
Situ
Boston, Massachusetts